IBM WebSphere

Application Server

Interview Questions

You'll Most Likely Be Asked

Job Interview Questions Series

 Vibrant Publishers

www.vibrantpublishers.com

IBM WebSphere Application Server
Interview Questions You'll Most Likely Be Asked

ISBN-10: 1468170996
ISBN-13: 978-14-68170-99-3

Library of Congress Control Number: 2012900421

This publication is designed to provide accurate and authoritative information in regard to the subject matter covered. The author has made every effort in the preparation of this book to ensure the accuracy of the information. However, information in this book is sold without warranty either expressed or implied. The Author or the Publisher will not be liable for any damages caused or alleged to be caused either directly or indirectly by this book.

Vibrant Publishers books are available at special quantity discount for sales promotions, or for use in corporate training programs. For more information please write to **bulkorders@vibrantpublishers.com**

Please email feedback / corrections (technical, grammatical or spelling) to **spellerrors@vibrantpublishers.com**

To access the complete catalogue of Vibrant Publishers, visit **www.vibrantpublishers.com**

Contents

This page is intentionally left blank

IBM WebSphere Application Server Interview Questions

Review these typical interview questions and think about how you would answer them. Read the answers listed; you will find best possible answers along with strategies and suggestions.

This page is intentionally left blank

Administration

1: When you use migration wizard (PMT) for WebSphere Application Server 8, do you expect to have all profile services up and running again?

Answer:

No, migration wizard only provides minimal function and it does not enable any services by default.

2: In a scenario where an administrator needs to migrate the entire application server profiles from v6.1 to v8 using Profile Management Tool (PMT) and he wants to keep all windows services created for these profiles, how to make sure that these windows services are kept after migration process?

Answer:

Administrator must create the new profile with a services enabled before starting the wizard, and then point to that profile during the migration wizard.

3: Assume that you installed WAS 6 after WAS 8 on your server, is it then possible to migrate WAS 6 nodes to WAS 8?

Answer:

No, it will not work as WAS 8 should be installed after those earlier versions.

4: What are the new capabilities in IBM Installation Manager V8?

Answer:

Here is a list of new capabilities:

    a) A single installation technology for installing and

uninstalling product

b) Updating and rolling back fixpacks and iFixes

c) Installing and uninstalling feature packs

d) GUI interface to perform individual operations; response files can be recorded either from the GUI or created by specifying the appropriate XML file for silent installation purposes

e) Silent mode support for invoking multiple operations.

5: Can you check on installed servers in ".nifregistry" file after installing WAS 8?
Answer:
No, WAS 8 is no longer using this registry file.

6: Is it possible to install WebSphere Application Server v5 over system i remotely?
Answer:
No, you can't as there is no GUI interface for version 5.

7: What may cause installation of WebSphere Application Server over system i to be stopped suddenly with no log file creation?
Answer:
Undefined host name for your system i box

8: What may cause problem in profile creation?
Answer:
Including special characters in your local host name may cause

problem in profile creation.

9: How can you administer your application server?

Answer:

Application server can be administered using admin console and wsadmin.

10: Can you federate a profile using manageprofiles command facility?

Answer:

No, you can't but you can delete a profile by manageprofiles command facility.

11: Will there be any problem in installing the application server on a target platform where it has been done before?

Answer:

Yes, it will cause an unattended installation of the application server.

12: Can you enable SSO for application server over system i?

Answer:

Yes, you can, during profile creation wizard.

13: Can you federate a node on system i box into dmgr over Windows/Linux platform?

Answer:

Yes, you can, as long as system i box can be accessed through network.

14: Can you use IIM for installing application server 8 over system i?

Answer:

No, you can't. You have to install it using QShell command line.

15: Can you take a copy of SystemOut.log files over system i while it is running?

Answer:

No, you can't as this file is locked by application server process.

16: Is there any other way to administer your application server over system i rather than its admin console?

Answer:

Yes, you can administer it using HTTPAdmin console.

17: How can an administrator make sure that application mapping between web server and application server was successful?

Answer:

It can be verified by viewing plug-in config file and making sure that the URI element under URI Group has a name attribute which is equal to the context root of that application.

18: What is the best way to avoid port conflict when adding a member to a cluster?

Answer:

Port conflict can be avoided by selecting option of generating unique HTTP ports.

19: Specify three ways to federate a node to a cell.

Answer:

It can be done using admin console, addnode command and using profile management tool (PMT).

20: How can an administrator make sure that every HTTP session is replicated to all members in the cluster?

Answer:

An administrator can make sure that every HTTP session is replicated to all members in the cluster by setting the number of replicas to the entire domain in the replication domain settings for the cluster.

21: What an administrator should do in order to administer an apache web server on a remote machine using dmgr?

Answer:

He should configure web server definition and configure a managed node on the remote host.

22: Can you install fix packs using Centralized Installation Manager (CIM)?

Answer:

Yes, but administrator must download the update installer for the appropriate platform into CIM repository.

23: How to manage multiple stand-alone application servers on different hosts?

Answer:

Multiple stand alone application servers can be managed by using a job manager through administrator agents.

24: How can you describe the relationship between a flexible management topology and the network deployment cell?

Answer:

Flexible management topology can be an alternative to the network deployment cell.

25: How to remove the application-scoped resources from an enhanced EAR file?

Answer:

Application scoped resources can be removed from an enhanced EAR file by removing META—INF/ibmconfig directory.

26: Is it possible to manage SIBus using fine-grained administrative security?

Answer:

No, SIBus messaging engine cannot be managed by fine-grained administration.

27: How to protect servlets in Java EE applications?

Answer:

Servlets can be protected by method permissions.

28: In order to modify the configuration of an enterprise application, through which components can the system admin make modification using wsadmin?

Answer:

Job manager or deployment manager

29: Where can administrator find binding information for an application?

Answer:

The administrator can find the binding information in the deployment descriptor.

30: State the three ways to enable verbose GC.

Answer:

   a) wsadmin script,
   b) -verbose:gc command line attribute and
   c) -Xoptionsfile command line option

31: What is the required configuration information to connect JMS destination to SIBus?

Answer:

JMS provider type, bus name and the bus destination

32: A scenario of a network deployment cell has one cluster and an application uses JMS client required to be deployed to the cluster, what are the required steps to be followed by administrator to make clients able to consume messages?

Answer:

The cluster must be added as a member to the Service Integration Bus (SIBus).

33: When does administrator need to create a JDBC provider?

Answer:

If the administrator is implementing an application which requires a connection to the database then he needs to create a JDBC provider.

34: How can administrator assign Java EE 5 security permissions to actual users in WebSphere Application Server?

Answer:

The administrator can assign security permissions to actual users by mapping application roles to users or groups in the WebSphere user registry.

35: What are the resources' scopes that may be taken into consideration by an administrator in order to create a security plan of using multiple security domains in that cell?

Answer:

Nodes, Servers and clusters

36: Which role is required in order to configure auditing in a WebSphere cell?

Answer:

An administrator account that has auditor access role

37: In a scenario where security is enabled using file based repository during the installation and the administrator needs to change administrator password, what shall the administrator do?

Answer:

He can change the primary administrator user password by configuring the federated repositories realm using admin console.

38: What is the use of Load Balancer?

Answer:

It is used in distributing HTTP Incoming traffic between multiple web servers.

39: Which type of servers is recommended to be placed in the demilitarized zone (DMZ)?

Answer:

Unmanaged HTTP servers

40: If it is required to deploy new application in the topology of an application server and unmanaged web server, what is required to be done by administrator in order to make this application accessed by this web server?

Answer:

Administrator has to manually propagate the plug-in configuration file to that web server.

41: How can administrators make sure that EJB client

requests are routed to the same node in case of multiple EJBs used by an application in a cluster?

Answer:

Administrators can ensure this by enabling the prefer local option in the cluster.

42: What are the types of dynamic caching service?

Answer:

Push and pull, Push only and Not shared

43: Which security role is required for your administrative console account in order to be able to assign new users to administrative tasks?

Answer:

Admin security manager role

44: Consider a scenario of a cluster containing two servers 1 and 2, the cluster is configured as a member of SIBus using high availability messaging policy, if Messaging Engine ME for bus1 starts on server1, then server 1 crashes. What is the expected behavior for that ME on bus1?

Answer:

ME for bus1 will start then on server2.

45: Is it possible to manage JVM thread pool by WebSphere Application Server?

Answer:

It is not possible but you can manage others like Web and ORB

Containers thread pools.

46: Is there any restriction on the installation path length for WebSphere using Windows OS?
Answer:

Yes, The maximum path length is 60 characters.

47: Will there be any change in the installation logs for Linux OS after finishing installation?
Answer:

Yes, logs under /root/waslogs will be moved to /opt/IBM/WebSphere/AppServer/logs/install.

48: Can you modify the deployment descriptor extension parameters using admin console or scripting in V6?
Answer:

No, it is not possible and the only way is to manually edit the file: ibm-web-ext.xmi.

49: Do you expect any problems during installation of WebSphere Application Server on Ubuntu?
Answer:

Yes, as Ubuntu is not a supported OS.

50: Is there any restriction on the user's privileges in WebSphere Application Server installation on Linux OS?
Answer:

No, but it is recommended to use the root account.

51: Can you schedule IIM instance installation for system z for a certain time after working hours?
Answer:
Yes, by submitting the installation job in batch mode.

52: How can you start WebSphere Application Server for system i?
Answer:
You can start it either using HTTP Admin console - port 2001 - or using Shell command.

53: Is it possible to start/stop your application server using HTTP server for system i?
Answer:
Yes, by mapping your application server start/stop to HTTP server's start/stop using HTTP Admin console - port 2001.

54: What are the required steps to be done by administrator to install the fix pack 35 for WebSphere Application Server 6.1 on system i?
Answer:
Administrator has to download the required fixes, then install them via "go licpgm" menu and then invoke "installFixPack61035" under its bin directory to complete the installation.

55: What are the supported java virtual machines on system i?
Answer:

Classic, 32-bits and 64-bits java virtual machines

56: Is Hung Thread Interrupter supported on system i?

Answer:

No, it is only supported on Microsoft Windows, Linux, IBM AIX, and IBM z/OS.

57: Can you install WebSphere Application Server using non-root users?

Answer:

Yes, you can but it is recommended to use root account then run change owner "chown" command for installation directory if you want to keep them away from any other users with low privileges.

58: How to make sure that your application server started?

Answer:

Check SystemOut.log file for "server is ready"

59: Can you install multiple versions of WebSphere Application Servers on a single box?

Answer:

Yes, but you may face port conflicts in case of version 8.

60: Which services will be affected if administrator turned off Data Replication Services (DRS)?

Answer:

Stateful session EJB persistence and failover, HTTP session

persistence and failover and dynamic caching replication services

61: What should be changed if the security credential for the external resource authentication changed?

Answer:

The J2C authentication data

62: Is it possible to use several different LDAP directory servers for WebSphere security?

Answer:

Yes, by configuring federated repositories including all LDAP directory servers.

63: Which new tool in version 8 is used to edit and configure either web servers or their plug-ins?

Answer:

WebSphere configuration toolkit (WCT). It is a centralized tool in order to maintain everything about web servers and their plug-ins.

64: Is it possible to deploy applications via drag/drop into a special directory in version 8?

Answer:

Yes, you can, by enabling this feature using administrative console as following: Click "Global deployment Settings" from the Applications section of the Left-Hand-Side navigation menu then Check the "Monitor directory to automatically deploy applications" then Specify desired directory and then save configurations.

65: Is it possible to delete Datasource and JDBCProvider using wsadmin in WAS 8?

Answer:

Yes, as these commands are recently supported as subset of "adminTask" commands.

66: What are the three resources associated with Java Messaging Service (JMS)?

Answer:

a) A connection factory,

b) Queue and

c) Activation specifications

67: If it is required to create additional persistent bindings of objects associated with a node for a certain application, what is the type of namespace portion you can bind those objects to?

Answer:

Node persistent

68: In a cluster cluster1 which has a configured memory to memory HTTP session replication, how can the administrator make sure that these HTTP sessions are replicated to all members in cluster1?

Answer:

It can be ensured by setting the number of replicas to entire domain of cluster1 under Environment and then Replication domains.

69: What do you know about session affinity?

Answer:

Session affinity is a way to guarantee that your request is handled by the same server and in case of a server crash in a clustered environment, another server will take this request over and the session will be retrieved and re-created for you transparently.

70: What is needed for recovering the transactions of a failed server?

Answer:

One of the failed server's peers needs to be able to take over the transaction logs from the failed server to recover its transactions.

71: What is the algorithm used in web server load balancer?

Answer:

"round-robin" algorithm. It is used for distributing the incoming requests between available resources according to a pre-defined weight for each resource.

72: Can you start administrative console of an application server after its federation into a dgmr?

Answer:

No, as this server is not a stand-alone anymore and its configuration files cannot be managed separately and can only be managed through dmgr admin console.

73: In a scenario where an administrator federated an application server into a cell and then he found that it was the wrong application server, how can he restore that stand alone server again?

Answer:

A configuration backup is taken during the process of "addnode" command so he can restore the stand-alone server again using this configuration backup.

74: How to avoid running "cleanupNode" command after removing a node?

Answer:

This can be done by using Force Delete button while running the"cleanupNode" command.

75: How to make sure that your application can be accessed via both web server's port and internal HTTP server's port?

Answer:

This can be ensured by mapping any new application during installation to both web server and internal HTTP server.

76: What are the two methods to enable session persistence?

Answer:

    a) Database sessions: It stores session data in an external database.

b) Memory-to-memory persistent sessions: It copies session data in the application server's memory across multiple application servers in a cluster.

77: What is the default administrative security repository type?
Answer:
File based federated repository

78: What are the two types of keys used in SSL?
Answer:
Symmetric and asymmetric keys

79: Is it possible to generate keys without using ikeyman for system i?
Answer:
Yes, from HTTP admin console via certificate manager.

80: How can administrators manage key rings for an application server?
Answer:
Administrators can manage key rings for an application server using admin console under Security, then SSL certificate and key management.

81: What is the purpose of caching proxy in edge component?
Answer:

Caching proxy helps to reduce network congestion within an enterprise by offloading security and content delivery from Web servers and Application Servers.

82: Can you enable trace without restart of the server?
Answer:

Yes, and you can enable it in the configuration as well.

83: If an administrator has tracing enabled for WebSphere Application Server, how can he use this tracing data for analysis?
Answer:

An administrator has to direct tracing output either to a dump file or to a memory ring buffer which dumps after trace stops.

84: How to manually trigger a thread dump for Linux/Unix?
Answer:

By using operating system facilities like "kill -3 <PID>" command or by using wsadmin to generate a thread dump via AdminControl administative task.

85: Can you change hung detection configuration using admin console?
Answer:

Yes, you can.

86: State the names of memory pools in Java process.
Answer:

Native and Java memory pools

87: How to avoid database binding issues in run time?

Answer:

Database binding issues can be avoided by using test connection button during deployment phase which will test the connection to database and reply whether the connection was successful or not.

88: What is connection pooling?

Answer:

Connection pooling is basically a pre-created connection to database in order to be used later by an application. It saves time as the application does not have to wait for the connection to be created.

89: What are the two types of connections in connection pooling?

Answer:

Shared connection pooling which is not released back to the pool even when connection is closed and unshared connection pooling which is released back to the pool when connection is closed.

90: What are the key connection pool parameters that you can control and adjust?

Answer:

Maximum number of connections and connection time out

91: Can you configure SSL between other components rather than between the browser and the web server?

Answer:

Yes, it can be configured between the plug-in and application server, application servers and LDAP servers.

92: What may cause deployment issues in an application?

Answer:

Corrupted EAR file or validation errors

93: While issuing startServer command, how many virtual machines are launched?

Answer:

Two virtual machines

94: Consider a scenario where an administrator had unsuccessful installation of WAS and he wants to reinstall it, what shall he do to get more information during next installation about the cause of the unsuccessful installation?

Answer:

Reinstall WAS with tracing turned on.

95: Which types of administrative tasks should be automated?

Answer:

Repetitive installation tasks and bulk changes

96: What is the default Garabage Collector (GC) policy?

Answer:

The default policy is to optimize for throughput "optthruput"

97: What are the types of clusters?

Answer:

Horizontal scaling, vertical scaling and a combination of both of them

98: What is cached using dynamic cache service?

Answer:

It caches the output of servlets, commands and JSPs.

99: What are the supported file types to be deployed/ using monitored directory deployment in WAS 8?

Answer:

EAR, WAR, JAR and SAR files

100: What are the supported actions by monitored directory deployment?

Answer:

Install, update and uninstall

101: How to control security of installing and uninstalling applications using monitored directory deployment feature in WAS 8?

Answer:

Administrator has to control permissions of copy and delete for the directory which is used for installing and uninstalling applications.

102: An administrator wants to install WebSphere Application Server v7 on a remote host, what is the best way to do this?

Answer:

Using Centralized Installation Manager (CIM) to add your installation target as following: Go to System Administrator then Centralized Installation Manager then Installation Targets and then Add Installation Target.

103: After installing all required operating system patches, what is the next step for an administrator to install WebSphere Application Server v7 on that remote host using CIM?

Answer:

Configuring an installation target for the remote host

104: How to make sure that your application server's installation was successful?

Answer:

The success of application server's installation can be ensured by using Installation Verification tool.

105: Assume that you are administering a cell which is configured to use LDAP server for authentication but other applications on this cell require authentication against file based registry, how can you manage this?

Answer:

Configure the global security to use LDAP registry and create another domain with a user realm for the file based registry and assign it to the desired applications.

106: When will it be required to generate deployment code for an application?

Answer:

Deployment code should be generated in case the application's EAR file contains a web service-enabled module.

107: If a single class loader is required for all the modules in all the enterprise applications on the application server, what should be done by administrator in order to apply this requirement?

Answer:

Set the classloader policy to single.

108: True or False: Resources that are defined at more specific scopes override duplicate resources that are defined at more general scopes?

Answer:

True

109: In a production environment, what shall an administrator do with sample applications which were installed with the server?

Answer:

He should disable these sample applications in order to avoid server hacking.

110: Assume that you have WebSphere Application Server and IIS web server, is it possible to make IIS acting as a web server for your application server?

Answer:

Yes, IIS can be used as a web server for WebSphere Application Server.

111: What is required to be done by an administrator before running migration wizard from a version to a newer one?

Answer:

Taking a full backup from your application server profiles is important before running migration wizard.

112: Can you manage migration from WebSphere Application Server v5 to v8?

Answer:

No, you can't migrate from v5 to v8; you have to migrate first from v5 to a next higher version then do the migration to v8.

113: Is there a way to migrate application servers from a version to another without using migration toolkit?

Answer:

Yes, using commands via command line which are WASPreUpgrade and WASPostUpgrade.

114: If you have two servers in a cluster, server1 and server2, server1 has a better CPU and memory resources, how can you direct more requests to server1?

Answer:

This is possible by setting higher weight value for server1 in the cluster configuration.

115: True or False: You can run Profile Management Tool by selecting System Administration and then selecting Run Profile Management Tool in the administrative console?

Answer:

False, you can run it either from command line or from first steps application.

116: What is the relevant command to backup WebSphere Application Server configuration and runtime settings?

Answer:

manageprofiles –backupProfiles –profile_name –backupFile backup_file_ name

117: An administrator would like to view web server plugin using administrative console, how can he manage this?

Answer:

From web server list, select target web server then in the properties menu click plug-in properties and click view.

118: Can you start and stop your application server using "first steps" application?

Answer:

No, you can only start the server using "first steps" application.

119: If an administrator didn't choose to create CIM repository in first installation of the application server but later he wants to use CIM, what shall he do?

Answer:

He can create CIM repository using installation factory as following: Launch the Installation Factory then Click Manage Repository for Centralized Installation Manager then enter the directory path to a WebSphere Application Server installation then enter the directory path to the repository and enter the directory path to an installation package and then Click Next.

120: Consider a scenario where a system administrator installed WebSphere Application Server but while using profile management tool, he didn't find the expected profile types, what could be the problem?

Answer:

It looks like the administrator installed the wrong package.

121: Consider a scenario where administrative security is enaled on dgmr and administrator needs to add a node to dmgr, will there be any extra parameters required in "addNode" command other than nodename?

Answer:

Yes, username and password parameters are required to authenticate to dmgr.

122: What are the two ways to manage the log archiving policies?

Answer:

The two ways to manage the log archiving policies are either by using log rotation or by setting the number of historical logs according to your storage.

123: A cluster member has suddenly crashed. The administrator is worried about the holding transaction locks in the database, what can he do to release these locks?

Answer:

Administrator has to verify another member in the cluster which has access to these transaction locks in order to recover the transactions of the failed server.

124: What are the functions provided by the caching proxy server?

Answer:

a) Dynamic content caching which reduces load of application's contents,

b) Reverse proxy configuration which makes the proxy server intercept user requests arriving from internet, forward them to the host and caching the returned data and

c) Content based routing function which routes requests based on rules that you write. The most common type is the content rule, which directs requests based on the path name in the URL.

125: Which services are implemented with WebSphere Application Server?

Answer:

Security, Naming, Transaction and Dynamic cache services

126: What is the type of archive file if an administrator is packing Session Initiation Protocol (SIP) servlets?

Answer:

SAR file

127: An administrator wants to change logging information level to provide more information, which level should be selected?

Answer:

Config level

128: What is the impact of selecting the check box of "pre-compile JSP" while deploying web module?

Answer:

Response time improvement for web clients

Problem Determination

129: What should an administrator do in order to analyze server hang problem?

Answer:

Administrator should analyze hang problem by triggering thread dumps for further analysis.

130: Based on the previous question, what is the effective way to collect this thread dump data?

Answer:

Wait till the hang happens then collect three thread dumps many seconds apart.

131: What is the best way to analyze your log files?

Answer:

The best way to analyze log files is by using IBM Support Assistant tool.

132: What are the services which are provided by IBM Support Assistant tool (ISA) for troubleshooting WebSphere Application Server problems?

Answer:

Remote debugging, data collection and file transfer

133: In case of OutOfMemory error, what is the best tool to analyze the problem?

Answer:

Memory Dump Diagnostic for Java

134: If an administrator suspects that there is a problem in JDBC connection pool, what tools should be used in such diagnostics?

Answer:

Tivoli Performance Viewer and Request Metrics

135: What is the function of the request metrics tool?

Answer:

Request metrics is a tool that enables you to track individual transactions, recording the processing time in each of the major WebSphere Application Server components.

136: What are the two types of problem detection monitoring?

Answer:

a) Passive monitoring which runs at all levels: network, OS, applications and mainly monitors the main system log files.

b) Active monitoring which runs beyond passive monitoring and it is the best way to check the health of the whole system by periodically sending an entire dummy transaction through the system and verify that it completes.

137: What do you know about FFDC (WAS v6.1)?

Answer:

FFDC stands for First Failure Data Capture which is always enabled and it captures details about exceptions reported in systemOut.log fil.

138: How can you enable tracing?

Answer:

Tracing can be enabled either by using administrative console or by using wsadmin.

139: How to view trace data?

Answer:

The trace data can be viewed using IBM Tivoli Log and Trace analyzer which is a part of IBM Support Assistant Tool. This tool enables you to import various log files as well as symptom databases against which log files can be analyzed and correlated.

140: What should be checked in the trace file in order to diagnose a connection issue?

Answer:

Trace files contain many parts; you have to search for "Connection leak logic" string in trace.log file for more information about the problem.

141: How to confirm that there is a security related issue while starting a server?

Answer:

Disable security using wsadmin command "securityoff" after opening connection with parameter "conntype NONE" then restart your application server and check if problem exists or not.

142: How to check for problems in web server?

Answer:

By checking its log files under <WAS_Dir>/logs folder.

143: Is it possible to trace IBM HTTP Server?

Answer:

Yes, by editing https.conf and changing LogLevel from warn to debug.

144: An administrator changed LogLevel on https.conf, will this take effect immediately?

Answer:

No, it requires a restart for the changes to take effect.

145: Is it possible to trace IBM HTTP Server plug-in?

Answer:

Yes, it is possible by editing plugin-cfg.xml and changing LogLevel from error to trace

146: An administrator changed LogLevel on IHS plugin, will this take effect immediately?

Answer:

No, a restart for the web server is required.

147: What may cause profile creation problems?

Answer:

a) File permission i.e. if the used user in profile creation has no access on WAS installation directory or

b) Problems with hostname i.e. if the server's host name contains invalid characters.

148: An administrator has Out Of Memory (OOM) errors in WebSphere Application Server logs, where should he start?
Answer:
Administrator has to enable verbose GC and then check native_stderr.log file for more information about this OOM error.

149: How to debug java heap exhaustion issues?
Answer:
Java heap exhaustion issues can be debugged using IBM Support Assistant tools like heap analyzer and memory analyzer

150: Is there any way to develop a tool to capture Out Of Memory errors?
Answer:
Yes, by using the JVM Tool Interface which is a new native programming interface. It provides a way to inspect the state and to control the execution of applications running the JVM.

151: Consider a scenario of a web application trying to access EJBs hosted on a cluster. The web application gives an exception of NameNotFoundException, what shall an administrator do?
Answer:

The administrator should use dumpNameSpace command to check if EJB's name is correct or not.

152: What should an administrator do to gather the required diagnostic trace data requested by IBM support team?

Answer:

Configure Diagnostic trace for the server and direct the output to a file then send this file to IBM support team.

153: What shall an administrator do in order to troubleshoot a communication problem between two nodes A and B within a cell which has security enabled? He guesses that there is a problem in signing certificate on node B?

Answer:

Verify that the CellDefaultTrustStore has the appropriate signing certificate in it then run syncNode on node B.

154: If you faced a problem in accessing your applications after a change in host name, what shall you do?

Answer:

You have to correct host name in "hosts" files on your OS and make sure that new host name is added to "virtual hosts" on your application server.

155: True or False: OutOfMemory errors are logged into SystemErr.log.

Answer:

True, you can use this information to start analyzing your

OOM errors.

156: Consider a scenario where you are able to access snoop servlet but you can't access your new deployed application, what could be the problem?

Answer:

The application is not mapped to the web server.

157: How to diagnose external web server's problems?

Answer:

Try to access your application using internal HTTP server of your application server. If it works then you have a problem in the web server.

158: How to troubleshoot connection problems between application server and database layer?

Answer:

This can be done by trying to connect to your database layer using any other stand-alone client. If it is working fine then the problem is in the connection between the application server and database layer.

159: How to check if client connection time out is too large or not for Windows OS?

Answer:

By using "netstat" command and monitoring if the connection status is changed to "closed" or not when your connection is closed by the application.

160: If you have OOM error and the .phd file is generated, what is the suitable tool to analyze this file?

Answer:

Memory Dump Diagnostic for Java (MDD4J)

161: In order to have trace data to be logged into a trace file, what should be done while configuring diagnostics trace service?

Answer:

Set the log detail level to fine, finer, finest or all.

This page is intentionally left blank

Scripting and Automation

162: What is the command used in backing up the profile configuration?

Answer:

backupConfig command

163: What is the wsadmin administrative object that is used to change static configuration objects?

Answer:

AdminConfig is used to change/create static configuration objects.

164: What is the wsadmin administrative object used to deploy applications?

Answer:

AdminApp is used to install/uninstall/list and edit applications.

165: What is the command used to execute script file using wsadmin?

Answer:

wsadmin –f <script_file>

166: What is the administrative object used to deploy applications?

Answer:

AdminApp object.

167: What is the administration object used in enabling

tracing?

Answer:

AdminConfig on configuration and AdminControl in runtime

168: Assume that you are new to wsadmin scripting and you need to automate some tasks but you don't know its syntax, what is the easiest way to get the correct syntax?

Answer:

While doing any task using administrative console, you can get the corresponding command by enabling the feature as follows: under "System administration" on left hand side click "Console Preferences" then check the box of "Enable command assistance notifications" and/or "Log command assistance commands" and then "Apply" changes.

169: In case you have Jacl scripts which have been used by other administrators and you are not familiar with Jacl language but you are familiar with Jython, will it be mandatory to rewrite all these scripts once again?

Answer:

No, you can use Jacl to Jython convert assistant in order to convert all of Jacl scripts to Jython ones.

170: How can administrators enable the collection of performance data of an application server using wsadmin scripts?

Answer:

You have to enable PMI data by invoking

"setInstrumentationLevel" operation on Perf MBean.

171: What is the correct command to use in order to save configuration changes in a Jython script file?

Answer:

AdminConfig.save()

Performance Tuning

172: Will there be any impact on the application server if FFDC is enabled?

Answer:

No, it will have no impact on the application server performance at all.

173: How to reduce server startup time and its memory footprint?

Answer:

It can be reduced by enabling the application server runtime provisioning.

174: An administrator needs to start the application server's web performance monitor over system i, will this cause any performance overload on your system?

Answer:

Yes, it will. So it is recommended to start it for a while then stop it again after getting the required information for the web performance advisor.

175: Will changes done using web performance advisor on application server for system i take effect immediately?

Answer:

No, you have to restart your application server in order to apply these changes.

176: In order to decrease the response time of a web application, what should an administrator do?

Answer:

Administrator has to enable and configure dynamic caching service from administrative console as following: Click Application servers then application_server and then Dynamic cache service.

177: How to monitor the health of any application server?

Answer:

The health of any application server can be monitored using Tivoli Performance View (TPV).

178: Is High Performance Extensible Logging (HPEL) enabled by default in version 8?

Answer:

No, you have to enable HPEL feature using administrative console before using it.

179: Consider a scenario that an administrator needs to use Performance Monitoring Infrastructure (PMI) tool and he already enabled PMI on the application server. What is the next step to collect performance data for this application server?

Answer:

An administrator has to start application server's monitoring using administrative console as following: under "Monitoring and Tuning" section on left hand side, select Current activity then select your server then "Start monitoring" for it.

180: What will happen when the JVM heap is too small?

Answer:

Applications require a minimum amount of memory to reach a stable state and this stable state occurs when the heap is no longer consistently growing. If the JVM is configured with a maximum heap that is too small, it will never allow the JVM to reach a stable state, then allocation failures will occur and the JVM will throw OutOfMemoryError.

181: If you have a memory leak issue, will increasing the maximum heap size fix the problem?

Answer:

No, it will only take a longer time till the problem occurs.

182: How to detect a connection management related issue in a connecting pooling?

Answer:

Connection management issues appear in SystemOut.log and SystemErr.log as error messages with prefix as J2CA or CWWJC or DSRA or WSCL or SQLException.

183: What is the impact of poor performance either from hardware side or from application's side on your business?

Answer:

More application support costs, loss of customer confidence and frequent upgrade of the hardware

184: Why do you need to do performance testing as early as

possible before going to production phase?

Answer:

To discover application's problems and to be able to fix them as much as you can before the application goes live.

185: What is the best period of the application life cycle to do performance testing?

Answer:

The design phase of the applications is the best phase to do performance testing.

186: True or False: Performance should not be considered after the design phase?

Answer:

False, it should be considered in all the phases of application including production phase.

187: Which tool is used in workload estimation for system i?

Answer:

IBM Systems WorkLoad estimator tool

188: What are the types of performance testing?

Answer:

a) Load testing which simulates anticipated user load and actual business operations and

b) Stress testing which evaluates performance at a level beyond estimated loads.

189: Which tool is used in performance testing?

Answer:

IBM Rational performance tester

190: Consider a scenario of a reported bad performance by end users, what are the categories which should be checked by administrator?

Answer:

Administrator has to check server's resources including memory and processor's usage and application's behavior by checking if there are idle database connections.

191: Which tools are used in performance monitoring and tuning?

Answer:

IBM Tivoli Monitoring and IBM Tivoli Composite Application Manager

192: How to tune java virtual machines?

Answer:

Java virtual machines can be tuned by tuning their garbage collector's intervals and associated heap sizes.

193: Is it mandatory to set the initial and maximum heap sizes to be the same?

Answer:

No, it is not mandatory. You can set different values but always keep initial value lower than the maximum value.

194: Is it recommended to tune all parameters at once?

Answer:

No, it is not recommended. You have to tune one parameter at a time to properly monitor any performance gain.

195: In order to check WebSphere application server response time on system i, what shall an administrator do?

Answer:

Using HTTP Admin console, he can check system response time and number of failed requests.

196: When is it recommended to use 64-bit JVM?

Answer:

It is recommended for applications which need very large heap size or large number of threads.

197: How to measure performance for your system i server?

Answer:

Performance Explorer and iDoctor tools are used to collect information about your system and then analyze the collected information.

198: Do you think that client side has any impact on your application's behavior?

Answer:

Yes, administrator has to work on client side performance tuning as many websites move their complex content from back-end servers to the client side using JavaScript or Flash.

199: Consider a scenario of a server which experiences a poor performance and after examining verbose GC data the administrator found that 80 KB objects cannot be allocated due to heap fragmentation, what action should be done by administrator to improve the performance?

Answer:

Increase the size of large object area (LOA) by adding - Xloainitial and -Xloamaximum to the Generic JVM Arguments in administrative console.

200: In order to enhance performance and speed messaging workload across multiple servers, what shall an administrator do?

Answer:

Deploy more than one messaging engine and link them together in a topology which has multiple interconnected service integration buses.

HR Questions

Review these typical interview questions and think about how you would answer them. Read the answers listed; you will find best possible answers along with strategies and suggestions.

1: Where do you find ideas?

Answer:

Ideas can come from all places, and an interviewer wants to see that your ideas are just as varied. Mention multiple places that you gain ideas from, or settings in which you find yourself brainstorming. Additionally, elaborate on how you record ideas or expand upon them later.

2: How do you achieve creativity in the workplace?

Answer:

It's important to show the interviewer that you're capable of being resourceful and innovative in the workplace, without stepping outside the lines of company values. Explain where ideas normally stem from for you (examples may include an exercise such as list-making or a mind map), and connect this to a particular task in your job that it would be helpful to be creative in.

3: How do you push others to create ideas?

Answer:

If you're in a supervisory position, this may be requiring employees to submit a particular number of ideas, or to complete regular idea-generating exercises, in order to work their creative muscles. However, you can also push others around you to create ideas simply by creating more of your own. Additionally, discuss with the interviewer the importance of questioning people as a way to inspire ideas and change.

4: Describe your creativity.

Answer:

Try to keep this answer within the professional realm, but if you have an impressive background in something creative outside of your employment history, don't be afraid to include it in your answer also. The best answers about creativity will relate problem-solving skills, goal-setting, and finding innovative ways to tackle a project or make a sale in the workplace. However, passions outside of the office are great, too (so long as they don't cut into your work time or mental space).

5: Tell me about a time when you worked additional hours to finish a project.

Answer:

It's important for your employer to see that you are dedicated to your work, and willing to put in extra hours when required or when a job calls for it. However, be careful when explaining why you were called to work additional hours – for instance, did you have to stay late because you set goals poorly earlier in the process? Or on a more positive note, were you working additional hours because a client requested for a deadline to be moved up on short notice? Stress your competence and willingness to give 110% every time.

6: Tell me about a time when your performance exceeded the duties and requirements of your job.

Answer:

If you're a great candidate for the position, this should be an easy question to answer – choose a time when you truly went above and beyond the call of duty, and put in additional work or voluntarily took on new responsib-ilities. Remain humble, and express gratitude for the learning opportunity, as well as confidence in your ability

to give a repeat performance.

7: What is your driving attitude about work?
Answer:

There are many possible good answers to this question, and the interviewer primarily wants to see that you have a great passion for the job and that you will remain motivated in your career if hired. Some specific driving forces behind your success may include hard work, opportunity, growth potential, or success.

8: Do you take work home with you?
Answer:

It is important to first clarify that you are always willing to take work home when necessary, but you want to emphasize as well that it has not been an issue for you in the past. Highlight skills such as time management, goal-setting, and multi-tasking, which can all ensure that work is completed at work.

9: Describe a typical work day to me.
Answer:

There are several important components in your typical work

day, and an interviewer may derive meaning from any or all of them, as well as from your ability to systematically lead him or her through the day. Start at the beginning of your day and proceed chronologically, making sure to emphasize steady productivity, time for review, goal-setting, and prioritizing, as well as some additional time to account for unexpected things that may arise.

10: Tell me about a time when you went out of your way at your previous job.

Answer:

Here it is best to use a specific example of the situation that required you to go out of your way, what your specific position would have required that you did, and how you went above that. Use concrete details, and be sure to include the results, as well as reflection on what you learned in the process.

11: Are you open to receiving feedback and criticisms on your job performance, and adjusting as necessary?

Answer:

This question has a pretty clear answer – yes – but you'll need to display a knowledge as to why this is important. Receiving feedback and criticism is one thing, but the most important part of that process is to then implement it into your daily work. Keep a good attitude, and express that you always appreciate constructive feedback.

12: What inspires you?

Answer:

You may find inspiration in nature, reading success stories, or mastering a difficult task, but it's important that your inspiration is positively-based and that you're able to listen and tune into it when it appears. Keep this answer generally based in the professional world, but where applicable, it may stretch a bit into creative exercises in your personal life that, in turn, help you in achieving career objectives.

13: How do you inspire others?

Answer:

This may be a difficult question, as it is often hard to discern the effects of inspiration in others. Instead of offering a specific example of a time when you inspired someone, focus on general principles such as leading by example that you employ in your professional life. If possible, relate this to a quality that someone who inspired you possessed, and discuss the way you have modified or modeled it in your own work.

14: What is customer service?

Answer:

Customer service can be many things – and the most important consideration in this question is that you have a creative answer. Demonstrate your ability to think outside the box by offering a confident answer that goes past a basic definition, and that shows you have truly considered your own individual view of what it means to take care of your customers. The thoughtful consideration you hold for customers will speak for itself.

15: Tell me about a time when you went out of your way for a customer.

Answer:

It's important that you offer an example of a time you truly went out of your way – be careful not to confuse something that felt like a big effort on your part, with something your employer would expect you to do anyway. Offer an example of the customer's problems, what you did to solve it, and the way the customer responded after you took care of the situation.

16: How do you gain confidence from customers?

Answer:

This is a very open-ended question that allows you to show your customer service skills to the interviewer. There are many possible answers, and it is best to choose something that you've had great experience with, such as "by handling situations with transparency," "offering rewards," or "focusing on great communication." Offer specific examples of successes you've had.

17: Tell me about a time when a customer was upset or agitated – how did you handle the situation?

Answer:

Similarly to handling a dispute with another employee, the most important part to answering this question is to first set up the scenario, offer a step-by-step guide to your particular conflict resolution style, and end by describing the way the conflict was resolved. Be sure that in answering questions about your own conflict resolution style, that you emphasize the importance of open communication and understanding from both parties, as well as a willingness to reach a compromise or other solution.

18: When can you make an exception for a customer?
Answer:

Exceptions for customers can generally be made when in accordance with company policy or when directed by a supervisor. Display an understanding of the types of situations in which an exception should be considered, such as when a customer has endured a particular hardship, had a complication with an order, or at a request.

19: What would you do in a situation where you were needed by both a customer and your boss?
Answer:

While both your customer and your boss have different needs of you and are very important to your success as a worker, it is always best to try to attend to your customer first – however, the key is explaining to your boss why you are needed urgently by the customer, and then to assure your boss that you will attend to his or her needs as soon as possible (unless it's absolutely an urgent matter).

20: What is the most important aspect of customer service?
Answer:

While many people would simply state that customer satisfaction is the most important aspect of customer service, it's important to be able to elaborate on other important techniques in customer service situations. Explain why customer service is such a key part of business, and be sure to expand on the aspect that you deem to be the most important in a way that is reasoned and well-thought out.

21: Is it best to create low or high expectations for a customer?
Answer:

You may answer this question either way (after, of course, determining that the company does not have a clear opinion on the matter). However, no matter which way you answer the question, you must display a thorough thought process, and very clear reasoning for the option you chose. Offer pros and cons of each, and include the ultimate point that tips the scale in favor of your chosen answer.

22: Why did you choose your college major?
Answer:

It's important to display interest in your work, and if your major is related to your current field, it will be simple for you to relate the two. Perhaps you even knew
while in college that you wanted to do a job similar to this position, and so you chose the major so as to receive the education and training you needed to succeed. If your major

doesn't relate clearly, it's still important to express a sense of passion for your choice, and to specify the importance of pursuing something that matters to you – which is how you made the decision to come to your current career field instead.

23: Tell me about your college experience.

Answer:

It's best to keep this answer positive – don't focus on parties, pizza, or procrastinating. Instead, offer a general summary of the benefits you received in college, followed by an anecdote of a favorite professor or course that opened up your way of thinking about the field you're in. This is a great opportunity for you to show your passion for your career, make sure to answer enthusiastically and confidently.

24: What is the most unique thing about yourself that you would bring to this position?

Answer:

This question is often asked as a close to an interview, and it gives you a final chance to highlight your best qualities to the employer. Treat the question like a sort of review, and explain why your specific mix of education, experience, and passions will be the ideal combination for the employer. Remain confident but humble, and keep your answer to about two minutes.

25: How did your last job stand up to your previous expectations of it?

Answer:

While it's okay to discuss what you learned if you expected too much out of a previous job, it's best to keep this question away from negative statements or portrayals. Focus your answer around what your previous job did hold that you had expected, and how much you enjoyed those aspects of the position.

26: How did you become interested in this field?

Answer:

This is the chance for you to show your passion for your career – and the interviewer will be assured that you are a great candidate if it's obvious that you enjoy your job. You can include a brief anecdote here in order to make your interest personal, but be sure that it is *brief*. Offer specific names of mentors or professors who aided in your discovery, and make it clear that you love what you do.

27: What was the greatest thing you learned while in school?

Answer:

By offering a lesson you learned outside of the classroom, you can show the interviewer your capacity for creativity, learning, and reflection. The practical lessons you learned in the classroom are certainly invaluable in their own right and may pertain closely to the position, but showing the mastery of a concept that you had to learn on your own will highlight your growth potential.

28: Tell me about a time when you had to learn a different skill set for a new position.

Answer:

Use a specific example to describe what you had to learn and how you set about outlining goals and tasks for yourself. It's important to show that you mastered the skill largely from your dedication to learning it, and because of the systematic approach you took to developing and honing your individual education. Additionally, draw connections between the skill you learned and the new position, and show how well prepared you are for the job.

29: Tell me about a person who has been a great influence in your career.

Answer:

It's important to make this answer easy to relate to – your story should remind the interviewer of the person who was most influential in his or her own career. Explain what you learned from this person and why they inspired you, and how you hope to model them later in your career with future successes.

30: What would this person tell me about you?

Answer:

Most importantly, if this person is one of your references – they had better know who you are! There are all too many horror stories of professors or past employers being called for a reference, and not being able to recall when they knew you or why you were remarkable, which doesn't send a very positive message to potential employers. This person should remember you as being enthusiastic, passionate, and motivated to learn and succeed.

31: What is the most productive time of day for you?
Answer:
This is a trick question – you should be equally productive all day! While it's normal to become extra motivated for certain projects, and also true that some tasks will require additional work, be sure to emphasize to the interviewer that working diligently throughout the entirety of the day comes naturally to you.

32: What was the most responsibility you were given at your previous job?
Answer:
This question provides you with an opportunity to elaborate on responsibilities that may or may not be on your resume. For instance, your resume may not have allowed room to discuss individual projects you worked on that were really outside the scope of your job responsibilities, but you can tell the interviewer here about the additional work you did and how it translated into new skills and a richer career experience for you.

33: Do you believe you were compensated fairly at your last job?
Answer:

Remember to stay positive, and to avoid making negative comments about your previous employer. If you were not compensated fairly, simply state that you believe your qualities and experience were outside the compensation limitations of the old job, and that you're looking forward to an opportunity that is more in line with the place you're at in your career.

34: Tell me about a time when you received feedback on your work, and enacted it.

Answer:

Try to give an example of feedback your received early in your career, and the steps you took to incorporate it with your work. The most important part of this question is to display the way you learned from the feedback, as well as your willingness to accept suggestions from your superiors. Be sure to offer reflection and understanding of how the feedback helped your work to improve.

35: Tell me about a time when you received feedback on your work that you did not agree with, or thought was unfair. How did you handle it?

Answer:

When explaining that you did not agree with particular feedback or felt it was unfair, you'll need to justify tactfully why the feedback was inaccurate. Then, explain how you communicated directly with the person who offered the feedback, and, most importantly, how you listened to their response, analyzed it, and then came to a mutual agreement.

36: What was your favorite job, and why?

Answer:

It's best if your favorite job relates to the position you're currently applying for, as you can then easily draw connections between why you enjoyed that job and why you are interested in the current position. Additionally, it is extremely important to explain why you've qualified the particular job as your favorite, and what aspects of it you would look for in another job, so that the interviewer can determine whether or not you are a good fit.

37: Tell me about an opportunity that your last position did not allow you to achieve.

Answer:

Stay focused on the positive, and be understanding of the limitations of your previous position. Give a specific example of a goal or career objective that you were not able to achieve, but rather than expressing disappointment over the missed opportunity, discuss the ways you're looking forward to the chance to grow in a new position.

38: Tell me about the worst boss you ever had.

Answer:

It's important to keep this answer brief, and positively focused. While you may offer a couple of short, critical assessments of your boss, focus on the things you learned from working with such an individual, and remain sympathetic to challenges the boss may have faced.

39: What is the best way for a company to advertise?
Answer:

If you're going for a position in any career other than marketing, this question is probably intended to demonstrate your ability to think critically and to provide reflective support for your answers. As such, the particular method you choose is not so important as why you've chosen it. For example, word of mouth advertising is important because customers will inherently trust the source, and social media advertising is important as it reaches new customers quickly and cheaply.

40: Is it better to gain a new customer or to keep an old one?
Answer:

In almost every case, it is better to keep an old customer, and it's important that you are able to articulate why this is. First, new customers generally cost companies more than retaining old ones does, and new customers are more likely to switch to a different company. Additionally, keeping old customers is a great way to provide a stable backbone for the company, as well as to also gain new customers as they are likely to recommend your company to friends.

41: What is the best way to win clients from competitors?
Answer:

There are many schools of thought on the best way to win clients from competitors, and unless you know that your interviewer adheres to a specific thought or practice, it's best to keep this question general. Rather than using absolute language, focus on the benefits of one or two strategies and show a clear, critical understanding of how these ways can succeed in a practical application.

42: How do you feel about companies monitoring internet usage?

Answer:

Generally speaking, most companies will monitor some degree of internet usage over their employees – and during an interview is not the best time to rebel against this practice. Instead, focus on positive aspects such as the way it can lead to increased productivity for some employees who may be easily lost in the world of resourceful information available to them.

43: What is your first impression of our company?

Answer:

Obviously, this should be a positive answer! Pick out a couple key components of the company's message or goals that you especially identify with or that pertain to your experience, and discuss why you believe these missions are so important.

44: Tell me about your personal philosophy on business.

Answer:

Your personal philosophy on business should be well-thought out, and in line with the missions and objectives of the company. Stay focused on positive aspects such as the service it can provide, and the lessons people gain in business, and offer insight as to where your philosophy has come from.

45: What's most important in a business model: sales, customer service, marketing, management, etc.?

Answer:

For many positions, it may be a good strategy to tailor this answer to the type of field you're working in, and to explain why that aspect of business is key. However, by explaining that each aspect is integral to the function as a whole, you can display a greater sense of business savvy to the interviewer and may stand out in his or her mind as a particularly aware candidate.

46: How do you keep up with news and emerging trends in the field?

Answer:

The interviewer wants to see that you are aware of what's currently going on in your field. It is important that your education does not stop after college, and the most successful candidates will have a list of resources they regularly turn to already in place, so that they may stay aware and engaged in developing trends.

47: Would you have a problem adhering to company policies on social media?

Answer:

Social media concerns in the workplace have become a greater issue, and many companies now outline policies for the use of social media. Interviewers will want to be assured that you won't have a problem adhering to company standards, and that you will maintain a consistent, professional image both in the office and online.

48: Tell me about one of the greatest problems facing *X* *industry* today.

Answer:

If you're involved in your career field, and spend time on your own studying trends and new developments, you should be able to display an awareness of both problems and potential solutions coming up in the industry. Research some of the latest news before heading into the interview, and be prepared to discuss current events thoroughly.

49: What do you think it takes to be successful in our company?

Answer:

Research the company prior to the interview. Be aware of the company's mission and main objectives, as well as some of the biggest names in the company, and also keep in mind how they achieved success. Keep your answer focused on specific objectives you could reach in order to help the company achieve its goals.

50: What is your favorite part of working in this career field?

Answer:

This question is an opportunity to discuss some of your favorite aspects of the job, and to highlight why you are a great candidate for the particular position. Choose elements of the work you enjoy that are related to what you would do if hired for the position. Remember to remain enthusiastic and excited for the opportunities you could attain in the job.

51: What do you see happening to your career in the next 10 years?

Answer:

If you're plugged in to what's happening in your career now, and are making an effort to stay abreast of emerging trends in your field, you should be able to offer the interviewer several predictions as to where your career or field may be heading. This insight and level of awareness shows a level of dedication and interest that is important to employers.

And Finally Good Luck!

INDEX

IBM WebSphere Application Server Questions
Administration

1: When you use migration wizard (PMT) for WebSphere Application Server 8, do you expect to have all profile services up and running again?

2: In a scenario where an administrator needs to migrate the entire application server profiles from v6.1 to v8 using Profile Management Tool (PMT) and he wants to keep all windows services created for these profiles, how to make sure that these windows services are kept after migration process?

3: Assume that you installed WAS 6 after WAS 8 on your server, is it then possible to migrate WAS 6 nodes to WAS 8?

4: What are the new capabilities in IBM Installation Manager V8?

5: Can you check on installed servers in ".nifregistry" file after installing WAS 8?

6: Is it possible to install WebSphere Application Server v5 over system i remotely?

7: What may cause installation of WebSphere Application Server over system i to be stopped suddenly with no log file creation?

8: What may cause problem in profile creation?

9: How can you administer your application server?

10: Can you federate a profile using manageprofiles command facility?

11: Will there be any problem in installing the application server on a target platform where it has been done before?

12: Can you enable SSO for application server over system i?

13: Can you federate a node on system i box into dmgr over Windows/Linux platform?

14: Can you use IIM for installing application server 8 over system i?

15: Can you take a copy of SystemOut.log files over system i while it is running?

16: Is there any other way to administer your application server over system i rather than its admin console?

17: How can an administrator make sure that application mapping between web server and application server was successful?

18: What is the best way to avoid port conflict when adding a member to a cluster?

19: Specify three ways to federate a node to a cell.

20: How can an administrator make sure that every HTTP session is replicated to all members in the cluster?

21: What an administrator should do in order to administer an apache web server on a remote machine using dmgr?

22: Can you install fix packs using Centralized Installation Manager (CIM)?

23: How to manage multiple stand-alone application servers on different hosts?

24: How can you describe the relationship between a flexible management topology and the network deployment cell?

25: How to remove the application-scoped resources from an

enhanced EAR file?

26: Is it possible to manage SIBus using fine-grained administrative security?

27: How to protect servlets in Java EE applications?

28: In order to modify the configuration of an enterprise application, through which components can the system admin make modification using wsadmin?

29: Where can administrator find binding information for an application?

30: State the three ways to enable verbose GC.

31: What is the required configuration information to connect JMS destination to SIBus?

32: A scenario of a network deployment cell has one cluster and an application uses JMS client required to be deployed to the cluster, what are the required steps to be followed by administrator to make clients able to consume messages?

33: When does administrator need to create a JDBC provider?

34: How can administrator assign Java EE 5 security permissions to actual users in WebSphere Application Server?

35: What are the resources' scopes that may be taken into consideration by an administrator in order to create a security plan of using multiple security domains in that cell?

36: Which role is required in order to configure auditing in a WebSphere cell?

37: In a scenario where security is enabled using file based repository during the installation and the administrator needs to change administrator password, what shall the administrator do?

38: What is the use of Load Balancer?

39: Which type of servers is recommended to be placed in the demilitarized zone (DMZ)?

40: If it is required to deploy new application in the topology of an application server and unmanaged web server, what is required to be done by administrator in order to make this application accessed by this web server?

41: How can administrators make sure that EJB client requests are routed to the same node in case of multiple EJBs used by an application in a cluster?

42: What are the types of dynamic caching service?

43: Which security role is required for your administrative console account in order to be able to assign new users to administrative tasks?

44: Consider a scenario of a cluster containing two servers 1 and 2, the cluster is configured as a member of SIBus using high availability messaging policy, if Messaging Engine ME for bus1 starts on server1, then server 1 crashes. What is the expected behavior for that ME on bus1?

45: Is it possible to manage JVM thread pool by WebSphere Application Server?

46: Is there any restriction on the installation path length for WebSphere using Windows OS?

47: Will there be any change in the installation logs for Linux OS after finishing installation?

48: Can you modify the deployment descriptor extension parameters using admin console or scripting in V6?

49: Do you expect any problems during installation of

WebSphere Application Server on Ubuntu?

50: Is there any restriction on the user's privileges in WebSphere Application Server installation on Linux OS?

51: Can you schedule IIM instance installation for system z for a certain time after working hours?

52: How can you start WebSphere Application Server for system i?

53: Is it possible to start/stop your application server using HTTP server for system i?

54: What are the required steps to be done by administrator to install the fix pack 35 for WebSphere Application Server 6.1 on system i?

55: What are the supported java virtual machines on system i?

56: Is Hung Thread Interrupter supported on system i?

57: Can you install WebSphere Application Server using non-root users?

58: How to make sure that your application server started?

59: Can you install multiple versions of WebSphere Application Servers on a single box?

60: Which services will be affected if administrator turned off Data Replication Services (DRS)?

61: What should be changed if the security credential for the external resource authentication changed?

62: Is it possible to use several different LDAP directory servers for WebSphere security?

63: Which new tool in version 8 is used to edit and configure either web servers or their plug-ins?

64: Is it possible to deploy applications via drag/drop into a special directory in version 8?

65: Is it possible to delete Datasource and JDBCProvider using wsadmin in WAS 8?

66: What are the three resources associated with Java Messaging Service (JMS)?

67: If it is required to create additional persistent bindings of objects associated with a node for a certain application, what is the type of namespace portion you can bind those objects to?

68: In a cluster cluster1 which has a configured memory to memory HTTP session replication, how can the administrator make sure that these HTTP sessions are replicated to all members in cluster1?

69: What do you know about session affinity?

70: What is needed for recovering the transactions of a failed server?

71: What is the algorithm used in web server load balancer?

72: Can you start administrative console of an application server after its federation into a dgmr?

73: In a scenario where an administrator federated an application server into a cell and then he found that it was the wrong application server, how can he restore that stand alone server again?

74: How to avoid running "cleanupNode" command after removing a node?

75: How to make sure that your application can be accessed via both web server's port and internal HTTP server's port?

76: What are the two methods to enable session persistence?

77: What is the default administrative security repository type?

78: What are the two types of keys used in SSL?

79: Is it possible to generate keys without using ikeyman for system i?

80: How can administrators manage key rings for an application server?

81: What is the purpose of caching proxy in edge component?

82: Can you enable trace without restart of the server?

83: If an administrator has tracing enabled for WebSphere Application Server, how can he use this tracing data for analysis?

84: How to manually trigger a thread dump for Linux/Unix?

85: Can you change hung detection configuration using admin console?

86: State the names of memory pools in Java process.

87: How to avoid database binding issues in run time?

88: What is connection pooling?

89: What are the two types of connections in connection pooling?

90: What are the key connection pool parameters that you can control and adjust?

91: Can you configure SSL between other components rather than between the browser and the web server?

92: What may cause deployment issues in an application?

93: While issuing startServer command, how many virtual machines are launched?

94: Consider a scenario where an administrator had unsuccessful installation of WAS and he wants to reinstall it, what shall he do to get more information during next installation about the cause of the unsuccessful installation?

95: Which types of administrative tasks should be automated?

96: What is the default Garabage Collector (GC) policy?

97: What are the types of clusters?

98: What is cached using dynamic cache service?

99: What are the supported file types to be deployed/ using monitored directory deployment in WAS 8?

100: What are the supported actions by monitored directory deployment?

101: How to control security of installing and uninstalling applications using monitored directory deployment feature in WAS 8?

102: An administrator wants to install WebSphere Application Server v7 on a remote host, what is the best way to do this?

103: After installing all required operating system patches, what is the next step for an administrator to install WebSphere Application Server v7 on that remote host using CIM?

104: How to make sure that your application server's installation was successful?

105: Assume that you are administering a cell which is configured to use LDAP server for authentication but other applications on this cell require authentication against file based registry, how can you manage this?

106: When will it be required to generate deployment code for an application?

107: If a single class loader is required for all the modules in all the enterprise applications on the application server, what should be done by administrator in order to apply this requirement?

108: True or False: Resources that are defined at more specific scopes override duplicate resources that are defined at more general scopes?

109: In a production environment, what shall an administrator do with sample applications which were installed with the server?

110: Assume that you have WebSphere Application Server and IIS web server, is it possible to make IIS acting as a web server for your application server?

111: What is required to be done by an administrator before running migration wizard from a version to a newer one?

112: Can you manage migration from WebSphere Application Server v5 to v8?

113: Is there a way to migrate application servers from a version to another without using migration toolkit?

114: If you have two servers in a cluster, server1 and server2, server1 has a better CPU and memory resources, how can you direct more requests to server1?

115: True or False: You can run Profile Management Tool by selecting System Administration and then selecting Run Profile Management Tool in the administrative console?

116: What is the relevant command to backup WebSphere Application Server configuration and runtime settings?

117: An administrator would like to view web server plugin using administrative console, how can he manage this?

118: Can you start and stop your application server using "first steps" application?

119: If an administrator didn't choose to create CIM repository in first installation of the application server but later he wants to use CIM, what shall he do?

120: Consider a scenario where a system administrator installed WebSphere Application Server but while using profile management tool, he didn't find the expected profile types, what could be the problem?

121: Consider a scenario where administrative security is enaled on dgmr and administrator needs to add a node to dmgr, will there be any extra parameters required in "addNode" command other than nodename?

122: What are the two ways to manage the log archiving policies?

123: A cluster member has suddenly crashed. The administrator is worried about the holding transaction locks in the database, what can he do to release these locks?

124: What are the functions provided by the caching proxy server?

125: Which services are implemented with WebSphere Application Server?

126: What is the type of archive file if an administrator is packing Session Initiation Protocol (SIP) servlets?

127: An administrator wants to change logging information level to provide more information, which level should be selected?

128: What is the impact of selecting the check box of "pre-compile JSP" while deploying web module?

Problem Determination

129: What should an administrator do in order to analyze server hang problem?

130: Based on the previous question, what is the effective way to collect this thread dump data?

131: What is the best way to analyze your log files?

132: What are the services which are provided by IBM Support Assistant tool (ISA) for troubleshooting WebSphere Application Server problems?

133: In case of OutOfMemory error, what is the best tool to analyze the problem?

134: If an administrator suspects that there is a problem in JDBC connection pool, what tools should be used in such diagnostics?

135: What is the function of the request metrics tool?

136: What are the two types of problem detection monitoring?

137: What do you know about FFDC (WAS v6.1)?

138: How can you enable tracing?

139: How to view trace data?

140: What should be checked in the trace file in order to diagnose a connection issue?

141: How to confirm that there is a security related issue while starting a server?

142: How to check for problems in web server?

143: Is it possible to trace IBM HTTP Server?

144: An administrator changed LogLevel on https.conf, will this take effect immediately?

145: Is it possible to trace IBM HTTP Server plug-in?

146: An administrator changed LogLevel on IHS plugin, will this take effect immediately?

147: What may cause profile creation problems?

148: An administrator has Out Of Memory (OOM) errors in WebSphere Application Server logs, where should he start?

149: How to debug java heap exhaustion issues?

150: Is there any way to develop a tool to capture Out Of Memory errors?

151: Consider a scenario of a web application trying to access EJBs hosted on a cluster. The web application gives an exception of NameNotFoundException, what shall an administrator do?

152: What should an administrator do to gather the required diagnostic trace data requested by IBM support team?

153: What shall an administrator do in order to troubleshoot a communication problem between two nodes A and B within a cell which has security enabled? He guesses that there is a problem in signing certificate on node B?

154: If you faced a problem in accessing your applications after a change in host name, what shall you do?

155: True or False: OutOfMemory errors are logged into SystemErr.log.

156: Consider a scenario where you are able to access snoop servlet but you can't access your new deployed application, what could be the problem?

157: How to diagnose external web server's problems?

158: How to troubleshoot connection problems between application server and database layer?

159: How to check if client connection time out is too large or not for Windows OS?

160: If you have OOM error and the .phd file is generated, what is the suitable tool to analyze this file?

161: In order to have trace data to be logged into a trace file, what should be done while configuring diagnostics trace service?

Scripting and Automation

162: What is the command used in backing up the profile configuration?

163: What is the wsadmin administrative object that is used to change static configuration objects?

164: What is the wsadmin administrative object used to deploy applications?

165: What is the command used to execute script file using wsadmin?

166: What is the administrative object used to deploy applications?

167: What is the administration object used in enabling tracing?

168: Assume that you are new to wsadmin scripting and you need to automate some tasks but you don't know its syntax, what is the easiest way to get the correct syntax?

169: In case you have Jacl scripts which have been used by other administrators and you are not familiar with Jacl language but you are familiar with Jython, will it be mandatory to rewrite all these scripts once again?

170: How can administrators enable the collection of

performance data of an application server using wsadmin scripts?

171: What is the correct command to use in order to save configuration changes in a Jython script file?

Performance Tuning

172: Will there be any impact on the application server if FFDC is enabled?

173: How to reduce server startup time and its memory footprint?

174: An administrator needs to start the application server's web performance monitor over system i, will this cause any performance overload on your system?

175: Will changes done using web performance advisor on application server for system i take effect immediately?

176: In order to decrease the response time of a web application, what should an administrator do?

177: How to monitor the health of any application server?

178: Is High Performance Extensible Logging (HPEL) enabled by default in version 8?

179: Consider a scenario that an administrator needs to use Performance Monitoring Infrastructure (PMI) tool and he already enabled PMI on the application server. What is the next step to collect performance data for this application server?

180: What will happen when the JVM heap is too small?

181: If you have a memory leak issue, will increasing the maximum heap size fix the problem?

182: How to detect a connection management related issue in a connecting pooling?

183: What is the impact of poor performance either from hardware side or from application's side on your business?

184: Why do you need to do performance testing as early as possible before going to production phase?

185: What is the best period of the application life cycle to do performance testing?

186: True or False: Performance should not be considered after the design phase?

187: Which tool is used in workload estimation for system i?

188: What are the types of performance testing?

189: Which tool is used in performance testing?

190: Consider a scenario of a reported bad performance by end users, what are the categories which should be checked by administrator?

191: Which tools are used in performance monitoring and tuning?

192: How to tune java virtual machines?

193: Is it mandatory to set the initial and maximum heap sizes to be the same?

194: Is it recommended to tune all parameters at once?

195: In order to check WebSphere application server response time on system i, what shall an administrator do?

196: When is it recommended to use 64-bit JVM?

197: How to measure performance for your system i server?

198: Do you think that client side has any impact on your application's behavior?

199: Consider a scenario of a server which experiences a poor performance and after examining verbose GC data the administrator found that 80 KB objects cannot be allocated due to heap fragmentation, what action should be done by administrator to improve the performance?

200: In order to enhance performance and speed messaging workload across multiple servers, what shall an administrator do?

HR Questions

1: Where do you find ideas?

2: How do you achieve creativity in the workplace?

3: How do you push others to create ideas?

4: Describe your creativity.

5: Tell me about a time when you worked additional hours to finish a project.

6: Tell me about a time when your performance exceeded the duties and requirements of your job.

7: What is your driving attitude about work?

8: Do you take work home with you?

9: Describe a typical work day to me.

10: Tell me about a time when you went out of your way at your previous job.

11: Are you open to receiving feedback and criticisms on your job performance, and adjusting as necessary?

12: What inspires you?

13: How do you inspire others?

14: What is customer service?

15: Tell me about a time when you went out of your way for a customer.

16: How do you gain confidence from customers?

17: Tell me about a time when a customer was upset or agitated – how did you handle the situation?

18: When can you make an exception for a customer?

19 What would you do in a situation where you were needed by both a customer and your boss?

20: What is the most important aspect of customer service?

21: Is it best to create low or high expectations for a customer?

22: Why did you choose your college major?

23: Tell me about your college experience.

24: What is the most unique thing about yourself that you would bring to this position?

25: How did your last job stand up to your previous expectations of it?

26: How did you become interested in this field?

27: What was the greatest thing you learned while in school?

28: Tell me about a time when you had to learn a different skill set for a new position.

29: Tell me about a person who has been a great influence in your career.

30: What would this person tell me about you?

31: What is the most productive time of day for you?

32: What was the most responsibility you were given at your previous job?

33: Do you believe you were compensated fairly at your last job?

34: Tell me about a time when you received feedback on your work, and enacted it.

35: Tell me about a time when you received feedback on your work that you did not agree with, or thought was unfair. How did you handle it?

36: What was your favorite job, and why?

37: Tell me about an opportunity that your last position did not allow you to achieve.

38: Tell me about the worst boss you ever had.

39: What is the best way for a company to advertise?

40: Is it better to gain a new customer or to keep an old one?

41: What is the best way to win clients from competitors?

42: How do you feel about companies monitoring internet usage?

43: What is your first impression of our company?

44: Tell me about your personal philosophy on business.

45: What's most important in a business model: sales, customer service, marketing, management, etc.?

46: How do you keep up with news and emerging trends in the field?

47: Would you have a problem adhering to company policies on social media?

48: Tell me about one of the greatest problems facing X *industry* today.

49: What do you think it takes to be successful in our company?

50: What is your favorite part of working in this career field?

51: What do you see happening to your career in the next 10 years?

Some of the following titles might also be handy:

1. .NET Interview Questions You'll Most Likely Be Asked

2. 200 Interview Questions You'll Most Likely Be Asked

3. Access VBA Programming Interview Questions You'll Most Likely Be Asked

4. Adobe ColdFusion Interview Questions You'll Most Likely Be Asked

5. Advanced JAVA Interview Questions You'll Most Likely Be Asked

6. AJAX Interview Questions You'll Most Likely Be Asked

7. Algorithms Interview Questions You'll Most Likely Be Asked

8. Android Development Interview Questions You'll Most Likely Be Asked

9. Ant & Maven Interview Questions You'll Most Likely Be Asked

10. Apache Web Server Interview Questions You'll Most Likely Be Asked

11. ASP.NET Interview Questions You'll Most Likely Be Asked

12. Automated Software Testing Interview Questions You'll Most Likely Be Asked

13. Base SAS Interview Questions You'll Most Likely Be Asked

14. BEA WebLogic Server Interview Questions You'll Most Likely Be Asked

15. C & C++ Interview Questions You'll Most Likely Be Asked

16. C# Interview Questions You'll Most Likely Be Asked

17. C++ Internals Interview Questions You'll Most Likely Be Asked

18. CCNA Interview Questions You'll Most Likely Be Asked

19. Cloud Computing Interview Questions You'll Most Likely Be Asked

20. Computer Architecture Interview Questions You'll Most Likely Be Asked

21. Core JAVA Interview Questions You'll Most Likely Be Asked

22. Data Structures & Algorithms Interview Questions You'll Most Likely Be Asked

23. Data WareHousing Interview Questions You'll Most Likely Be Asked

24. EJB 3.0 Interview Questions You'll Most Likely Be Asked

25. Entity Framework Interview Questions You'll Most Likely Be Asked

26. Fedora & RHEL Interview Questions You'll Most Likely Be Asked

27. GNU Development Interview Questions You'll Most Likely Be Asked

28. Hibernate, Spring & Struts Interview Questions You'll Most Likely Be Asked

29. HTML, XHTML and CSS Interview Questions You'll Most Likely Be Asked

30. HTML5 Interview Questions You'll Most Likely Be Asked

31. IBM WebSphere Application Server Interview Questions You'll Most Likely Be Asked

32. iOS SDK Interview Questions You'll Most Likely Be Asked

33. Java / J2EE Design Patterns Interview Questions You'll Most Likely Be Asked

34. Java / J2EE Interview Questions You'll Most Likely Be Asked

35. Java Messaging Service Interview Questions You'll Most Likely Be Asked

36. JavaScript Interview Questions You'll Most Likely Be Asked

37. JavaServer Faces Interview Questions You'll Most Likely Be Asked

38. JDBC Interview Questions You'll Most Likely Be Asked

39. jQuery Interview Questions You'll Most Likely Be Asked

40. JSP-Servlet Interview Questions You'll Most Likely Be Asked

41. JUnit Interview Questions You'll Most Likely Be Asked
42. Linux Commands Interview Questions You'll Most Likely Be Asked
43. Linux Interview Questions You'll Most Likely Be Asked
44. Linux System Administrator Interview Questions You'll Most Likely Be Asked
45. Mac OS X Lion Interview Questions You'll Most Likely Be Asked
46. Mac OS X Snow Leopard Interview Questions You'll Most Likely Be Asked
47. Microsoft Access Interview Questions You'll Most Likely Be Asked
48. Microsoft Excel Interview Questions You'll Most Likely Be Asked
49. Microsoft Powerpoint Interview Questions You'll Most Likely Be Asked
50. Microsoft Word Interview Questions You'll Most Likely Be Asked
51. MySQL Interview Questions You'll Most Likely Be Asked
52. NetSuite Interview Questions You'll Most Likely Be Asked
53. Networking Interview Questions You'll Most Likely Be Asked
54. OOPS Interview Questions You'll Most Likely Be Asked
55. Oracle DBA Interview Questions You'll Most Likely Be Asked
56. Oracle E-Business Suite Interview Questions You'll Most Likely Be Asked
57. ORACLE PL/SQL Interview Questions You'll Most Likely Be Asked
58. Perl Interview Questions You'll Most Likely Be Asked
59. PHP Interview Questions You'll Most Likely Be Asked
60. PMP Interview Questions You'll Most Likely Be Asked
61. Python Interview Questions You'll Most Likely Be Asked
62. RESTful JAVA Web Services Interview Questions You'll Most Likely Be Asked
63. Ruby Interview Questions You'll Most Likely Be Asked
64. Ruby on Rails Interview Questions You'll Most Likely Be Asked
65. SAP ABAP Interview Questions You'll Most Likely Be Asked
66. Selenium Testing Tools Interview Questions You'll Most Likely Be Asked
67. Silverlight Interview Questions You'll Most Likely Be Asked
68. Software Repositories Interview Questions You'll Most Likely Be Asked
69. Software Testing Interview Questions You'll Most Likely Be Asked
70. SQL Server Interview Questions You'll Most Likely Be Asked
71. Tomcat Interview Questions You'll Most Likely Be Asked
72. UML Interview Questions You'll Most Likely Be Asked
73. Unix Interview Questions You'll Most Likely Be Asked
74. UNIX Shell Programming Interview Questions You'll Most Likely Be Asked
75. VB.NET Interview Questions You'll Most Likely Be Asked
76. XLXP, XSLT, XPath, XForms & XQuery Interview Questions You'll Most Likely Be Asked
77. XML Interview Questions You'll Most Likely Be Asked

For complete list visit
www.vibrantpublishers.com

NOTES

www.ingramcontent.com/pod-product-compliance
Lightning Source LLC
Chambersburg PA
CBHW071007050326
40689CB00014B/3527